Rainbow

Lily Lawson

THE
WRIGHT HOUSE

By The Author

Poetry

My Father's Daughter

A Taste of What's to Come

https://www.lilyswritinglife.com/

Rainbow's Red Poetry Book is named for
Lily's Instagram handle, Poetic Rainbow.

You will find me in moments of anger
I weave through hate and love.
My rebel strength will emerge,
defiant in the aftermath.
I welcome you to read my words,
may they speak their message

I am Red.

Contents

Parenting

Love was looking for their children.

Kindness was helping people.
Compassion was listening.
Understanding was mediating.
Faith was encouraging.
Hope was sharing joy.

Love stopped looking for their children;
they were out in the world making a difference,
as Love taught them.

Complexities of Human Existence

Questioning, doubting,
growing, learning,
loving, hurting, healing,
believing, accepting,
changing, developing, becoming.

Collective Creativity`

We paint from the palette of life –
use brushes of all sizes, old and new.
Sometimes other people
will add colours to the canvas.
Each image, unique in interpretation
Every one, a masterpiece.

Artistic Licence

To paint your portrait,
I attempt to capture
every nuance of your being.
As my brush strokes the canvas,
the palette is not enough
to do you justice.

Hate vs Love

Hate leaks from lips,
its powerful punch poisoning all within its
wake,
wasting weighty words on trivial pursuits.

Love flows from the heart,
its calming lotion pouring in caressing streams,
healing wounds, seeping into souls.

Hate's afflicted admirers
keen to ingratiate themselves
bow and scrape at its feet.
When they hear the battle cry, they charge.

Love listens long.
Its gentle voice persuading, reaching out,
accepting all in its embrace.

Awakening

The richness of this existence
catches me unawares,
from sorrow's depths
to heights of ecstasy.
The wideness of each experience,
the uniqueness of each moment.
Differences and similarities,
divide and intersect
between the humans I encounter.

We woke up this morning.
We have much to be grateful for.

Sunrise

When the first sign of light breaking
takes the darkness from my sight,
the dawn of early promise
shines in the blackened night.

When the shadows that you cast
are making themselves known,
my heart is thumping fast –
all my worries have just flown.

When the waters of the morning
are silent, still and calm.
The newness of day dawning
seems to shelter me from harm.

When it feels as though my world
will never be the same,
my very self exists
in the utterance of your name.

Answering the call

Music speaks
revealing emotions,
extracting memories.
Poetic words,
captured feelings,
released with every beat.
Without words,
notes speak
a language of their own.
My soul
hears each note anew.
My spirit responds,
alone or with another.
I have to dance.

Refuge

They arrive in their group,
knowing separation awaits them –
trusting their new homes
will be safe,
a place to be loved and cherished
as they were meant to be.

They will make friends
among their various companions.

They make their arduous journey.
Days passed with many strangers.
The life they knew abandoned.
They carry what possessions they can.
Their fate, their fellow travellers
and those they left behind
beyond their control.
Fate's dice roll separates life and death.

Arrival.

Journey's end.

In this alien landscape
they hope to make their home.

Perfection

Roses,
tempting,
beautiful aroma,
delicate flowers.

Thorns
reminding us
beautiful things
have flaws.

The Vault

History is buried deep within me.

Scared of excavation,
I reseal the vault,
unable to continue.

The contents of my vault cause me pain.

Constant re-examination dulls its sting.

Remaining memory fragments
grow brittle with increasing fragility,
damaged by years of neglect.

The treasures I wish to exhume
and cherish in future years –
the reason for my quest –
become more visible now.

My strength grows.

Excavation day has not been set.

It will come.

Isolation

Falling into the deep dark pit,
I reach for the safety rope.

It's cut with a knife.

Help is on its way they say,
I've heard this before
but no help came.

My climbing ability is impaired
by countless wounds.

The hope of full recovery,
recedes to a remote possibility.

The choice seems clear;
I have to save myself
again.

Abandon Ship

I wondered why they walked,
and not with you,
tattered ends of unfinished tasks
trailing in their wake.

Newcomers picked up the threads –
a wish to finish
the abandoned whole –
not to judge those gone before,
or even understand
why the clocks in this place chimed so slow.

Revelation starts to appear,
and I, too, walk,
but not with you.

Game Over

You won't destroy me.

You only hurt me
if I let you.

My sanity depends
on keeping you
out.

I guard my barriers
they are
manned,
patrolled,
there is no chance of sleep.

You sense every weakness.
You highlight them,
expose them.

Thrilling in making me look bad,
you gather up support.

I'm left to defend myself,
alone.

I walk away.

Your allies follow –
never to console –
to rip into me,
telling me
to apologise,
to you.

No matter what,
you play the victim.

No room for compassion.

No possibility you are wrong.

I leave the game,
it's over now,
I only played because I had to,
I don't have to any more.

Sanctuary

Here
things could be
the way they were.

Here
the temporary pause
before reality.

I need
to enter the real world
and begin.

The temptation
to stay here
and pretend.

I cherish
my moments,
fleeting as they are.

I need
to live but also
still to dream.

After William

As each takes their leave
another follows in their stead,
with scarce a beat between.
Each exit and each entrance
is controlled by one more powerful,
than all the players ever stood upon this stage
or yet to walk its hallowed boards.
And yet the deeds of men
shall be noted down.
That those yet to be
shall know the triumphs and disasters of the age
and reflect upon the whole.
That lives long spent will not wasted be.

A Shaft of Light

Positivity crept with its torch in the night.
Uncertainty walked alongside.
Human-made stars blinked in the dark.
Brightness growing as each minute passed by.
The way became clear –
it grew, blooming and basking in love.

No Surrender

You may hurt me,
or desert me,
or think you can bring me down.

No, not me.
I'm stronger than you think.
It would take more than you can throw at me.

I will survive.
I will thrive.
You will never win.

I will stand tall
through it all.
Bring it on.

Down But Not Out

This old thing's been through some action.
This old thing's been through some stuff.
There have been times they felt defeated,
because the going got quite rough.

This old thing just keeps on going,
gets back up and starts again.
Even when they're really hurting,
keeps on pushing through the pain.

This old thing won't throw the towel in,
because this old thing is tough.
They will survive whatever,
when others have had quite enough.

Hold On

When darkest night threatens to overtake,
hold on.

When you bend so much you fear you'll break,
hold on.

My hand's there within your reach.
Hold on.

No matter what I'll never preach.
Hold on.

Tomorrow waits in a different land.
Hold on.

You have people who understand.
Hold on.

Keep holding on.

Recipe for Life

Keep going.
See the best in people.
Look after yourself.
Be kind when you can.
Do no harm.
Avoid stress as much as possible.
Roll with curve balls.
Be aware of what matters and what doesn't.
Communicate.
Forgive.
Say thank you.
Apologise.
Laugh.
Love.
Hang out with people
who bring out the best in you.
Avoid those who bring out the worst in you.
Pay attention.
Keep learning.
Keep growing.
Be yourself.
Do your best.

Life is complicated, yet very simple.

Now you've read my book
don't forget to review
Amazon, Goodreads,
Bookbub too!
Thank you very much
I'm counting on you!

Lily x

By The Author

Poetry

My Father's Daughter

A Taste of What's to Come

Rainbow's Red Book of Poetry

https://www.lilyswritinglife.com/

Acknowledgements

Thank you for reading my book.

Writing is a solo activity. Writers and poets need people to help them navigate the trials and celebrate the joys which are part of that life. With that in mind – a few thank yous.

Thank you to everyone who follows me on social media or lilyswritinglife.com or receives my newsletter. I really appreciate the reactions, comments, and shares. It's good to know my writing strikes a chord.

Thanks to those of you who leave a book review. I know myself how valuable someone's opinion can be when considering trying out a new author or a new genre.

Thanks to the talented Ann Garcia for my amazing cover.

Thanks to Dreena for helping with the formatting.

Thanks to all at SPG for their help, support, and advice.

With special thanks to my readers –
Cheryl, Dreena, Becky, Alex, Jo, and Jay- sorry
it's not wine.

Thanks to all at Team Tea and Books –

Special thanks to my reader Lamia and to
Helen, Laura, Morgan, and Ash – sorry it's not
cake.

Thanks to all at Write Club. Special thanks to
my reader Cin for her support and
encouragement.

Thanks to all at Smile especially Clare for her
wisdom and understanding.

Thanks to the poets – Suzanne, Louise, Jane,
Karen, Tracy, Sharon, and Shell.

Thanks to Anita for believing I can fly and
encouraging me to do so.

Thanks to Ruth at AllFM for allowing me on
her show.

Thanks to Christine for her honest critiques
and her belief in me.

Thanks to Lady B. This book would still be a doc on my computer if it wasn't for her.

Thanks to Butterfly who unexpectedly flew into my life and made such a difference.

Thanks to everyone who has encouraged me to see it's ok to be me.

And finally, thanks to my Dad for everything.

By The Author

My Father's Daughter

'My Father's Daughter, a collection of poems ranging from light-hearted to heart-rending captures Lily Lawson's thoughtful observations about life and love.'

A Taste of What's to Come

A selection of accessible, relatable, eclectic poetry.
Each piece tells its story
in only the way Lily can.'

Rainbow's Red Book of Poetry
Weaving through love and hate,
I rise from the ashes, my words you own –
I am red.

**Something different,
an illustrated children's book.**

Santa's Early Christmas
Last year Santa was hungry and thirsty by the time he delivered all the presents. But when he came home there was no food and drink left! This year Santa decides things are going to be different.

A poem from

My Father's Daughter

The Modern World

Stop all the texts,
remove the mobile phone,
prevent the isolation
in spending time alone,
turn off the modem,
cease the internet,
go and make some memories
you will not forget.

Let Facebook miss you,
let the tweeting stop,
go do your shopping
in an actual shop,
put down the tablet,
put the kindles back,
start living dangerously;
read a paperback!

We used to call, to just converse,
now it seems that we find nothing worse.
Talking to voicemail or to answerphone,
we have our conversations on our own.

Libraries are not wanted now,
close up every door,
dare we venture in to loiter,
or to just explore?
Losing real connection,
deprived of human touch,
face to face meetings
have become too much.

About The Author

Lily Lawson is a poet and fiction writer living in the UK. She has poetry, short stories and creative non-fiction published in anthologies and online in addition to her books.

You can find out more about Lily and read more of her work on her blog. Subscribers to Life with Lily are the first to hear all her writing news. You can sign up here.

Printed in Great Britain
by Amazon